The Pilgrims First Year

by Linda Yoshizawa
illustrated by Rich Stergulz

PEARSON

Scott
Foresman

Editorial Offices: Glenview, Illinois • Parsippany, New Jersey • New York, New York
Sales Offices: Needham, Massachusetts • Duluth, Georgia • Glenview, Illinois
Coppell, Texas • Ontario, California • Mesa, Arizona

In the early 1600s, the Wampanoag people lived in the place we now call Massachusetts. These Native Americans knew how to live off the land. They were experts at hunting, fishing, farming, and gathering.

The Wampanoag used **resources** around them to make their clothing and build homes. They sewed clothes from deer and elk skins. They made homes from trees and grass.

In spring, the Wampanoag moved to the shore. They planted crops, fished, and gathered clams. In the fall, they moved inland and spent the winter in the forest.

In each place, the Wampanoag built their homes. They made the frames from long saplings, which are young trees. They made walls and floors from mats they wove from grass. When moving time came, the Wampanoag rolled up the frame sticks in the mats and carried them to a new place. Then they rebuilt their homes in the new location.

The Wampanoag lived on the shore during warm weather.

In the fall of 1620, the Wampanoag returned to their winter homes just as they had always done. They did not know that something was about to happen that would change their way of life forever.

A small ship was sailing toward North America. The people on the ship were searching for religious freedom, and they became known as Pilgrims.

The Pilgrims' ship was called the *Mayflower*. The small ship was crowded. There was not much food, and the weather was stormy. Many passengers grew ill. Two people died.

Finally, the *Mayflower* arrived at Plymouth, Massachusetts. It was December of 1620. The Pilgrims' long journey was over, but their new life was just beginning. What, they wondered, would the new year bring?

The *Mayflower* had to go through rough and stormy seas.

December was a tough time to arrive in New England. It was winter, and the Pilgrims did not have much food left. They did not know much about hunting. It was too late to plant crops. The Pilgrims settled into an empty Indian village. They started building their new homes.

Like the Wampanoag, the Pilgrims built homes with materials they found. They used wood from the forest. They covered their roofs with grass and reeds.

The Pilgrims did not invent new kinds of homes. They built homes similar to their old ones in England. Most had one large room with a smaller space above it. They had a fireplace for cooking and to heat the house.

Pilgrim homes in North America were built like their homes in England.

The Pilgrims had a hard first winter. Half of the people died. But when spring came and the *Mayflower* sailed back to England, none of the Pilgrims left. They had **faith** and hoped that they would have a better life. They were sure they would be able to make this new land their home.

Would the Pilgrims have been able to do this on their own? No one knows, because when spring came, help arrived with it.

A Native American named Squanto came to the village. Squanto spoke English. Unlike most of his people, Squanto had traveled outside of America. Sadly, when Squanto returned home from his travels, he found that his whole tribe had gotten sick and died.

Squanto then chose to live with the Wampanoag. When the Wampanoag told him about the Pilgrims, he joined the new colony. Squanto's knowledge helped the Pilgrims survive.

Follow the path of the *Mayflower* from England to New England and back again.

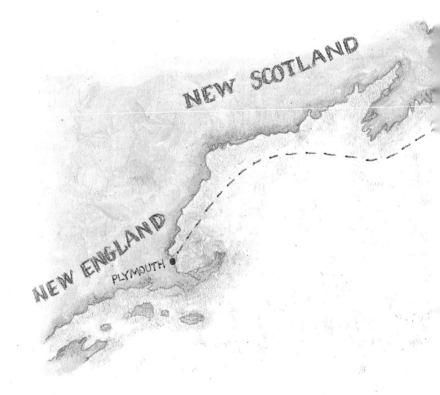

In their first year in America, the Pilgrims' most important job was planting crops. They did not want to go through another hungry winter.

Squanto taught the Pilgrims how to plant crops such as beans and squash. They learned to plant corn in mounds and to use fish as **fertilizer.**

The Wampanoag and the Pilgrims farmed in the summer. The Wampanoag lived as usual. The Pilgrims learned new ways to live in their new home.

Both groups spent much of their time doing chores. Everyone had to **participate.**

Wampanoag men showed the Pilgrim men how to hunt.

Wampanoag men and boys got food by hunting, fishing, and trapping. They made canoes, knives, bows, and arrows.

Pilgrim men and boys planted and harvested crops. Squanto taught them how to hunt, trap, and dig for clams.

Wampanoag girls worked with their mothers. They helped farm. They also gathered wild plants, such as berries. Then they made the meals. They made clothing and grass mats for their homes.

Pilgrim girls and women worked at cooking, cleaning, and washing clothes. They made candles, soap, and mattresses.

Both boys and girls had other chores too. They gathered wood for the fireplace. They carried water to the house and the fields. They looked after the younger children.

The girls helped their mothers make candles to light the house.

Even with all their chores, both Wampanoag and Pilgrim children had time left over to learn and play.

Neither group had schools, but both groups had important things to learn. Wampanoag children learned about nature. They also learned about their **traditions.**

Pilgrim children learned about their traditions too. They studied the religion of their parents. They learned to read, write, and do arithmetic.

The children in both groups played games. Wampanoag children ran races and practiced shooting with bows and arrows. They also played ball.

Pilgrim children also had fun outdoors. They played games such as marbles and board games.

The first Thanksgiving was held in October of 1621.

When the year 1621 was almost over, the Pilgrims looked around their new home. They liked what they saw, and they were thankful. The Pilgrims celebrated with a feast and invited their Wampanoag friends to **dine** with them. The feast lasted three days. There was plenty for everyone to eat. That harvest feast became the idea for the **holiday** we call Thanksgiving.

In 1621, the Pilgrims learned a lot from the Wampanoag. Perhaps the Wampanoag learned a few things from the Pilgrims too.

Now Try This

Two Ways to Remember History

In 1621, Pilgrims kept records by writing. The Wampanoag remembered history by retelling events aloud.

Imagine that you live in 1621. Think like a Pilgrim, or think like a Wampanoag. Write or tell your own story about the winter or spring of 1621.

If you choose to think like a Pilgrim. . .

1. Write a letter to a family member or friend you left behind in Europe.
2. Tell about the events.
3. Tell about your feelings.
4. Invite classmates to read your letter.

If you choose to think like a Wampanoag. . .

1. Think about how to retell what happened in 1621.
2. Practice telling about the events.
3. Tell what you thought of the new people who came to your land.
4. Sit in a circle with other storytellers and listen to each other's tales.

Glossary

dine *v.* to eat a meal.

faith *n.* a belief that something is possible.

fertilizer *n.* something that helps plants grow.

holiday *n.* a special celebration.

participate *v.* to join in.

resources *n.* useful materials.

traditions *n.* customs or beliefs handed down from parents to children.